Fact Finders ®

Kids' Translations

THE PLEDGE OF ALLEGIANCE

in Translation

What It Really Means

by **Elizabeth Raum**

Consultant:
Richard J. Ellis
Department of Politics
Willamette University
Salem, Oregon

Capstone
press ®

Mankato, Minnesota

Fact Finders is published by Capstone Press,
151 Good Counsel Drive, P.O. Box 669, Mankato, Minnesota 56002.
www.capstonepub.com

072011
006285R

Books published by Capstone Press are manufactured with paper
containing at least 10 percent post-consumer waste.

Library of Congress Cataloging-in-Publication Data
Raum, Elizabeth.
    The Pledge of Allegiance in translation: what it really means / by Elizabeth Raum.
    p. cm. — (Fact finders. Kids' translations)
    Includes bibliographical references and index.
    Summary: "Presents the full text of the Pledge of Allegiance in both its original version and in a translated version
using everyday language. Describes the events that led to the creation of the pledge
and its significance through history" — Provided by publisher.
    ISBN-13: 978-1-4296-1931-8 (hardcover)
    ISBN-10: 1-4296-1931-7 (hardcover)
    ISBN-13: 978-1-4296-2846-4 (softcover pbk.)
    ISBN-10: 1-4296-2846-4 (softcover pbk.)
    1. Bellamy, Francis. Pledge of Allegiance to the Flag — Juvenile literature. I. Title.
JC346.R38 2009
323.6'50973 — dc22
                                                              2007051304

Editorial Credits

Megan Schoeneberger, editor; Gene Bentdahl, set designer and illustrator; Wanda Winch, photo researcher

Photo Credits

Alamy/M Stock, 9
AP Images/Boston Public Library, copy photo, 5; Paul Sakuma, 25
Capstone Press/Karon Dubke, cover (boy), 7 (top), 11 (bottom), 28
Cleveland Colby Colgate Archives, Colby-Sawyer College, New London, New Hampshire, 14 (left), 15
Corbis, 21; Bettmann, 8, 18–19, 22
Courtesy of the Archives of the Upham Family Society, 17 (top)
Department of Rare Books and Special Collections, Rush Rhees Library, University of Rochester, cover, 4 (bottom), 6
    (bottom), 14 (right), 17 (bottom)
The Image Works/Bob Daemmrich, 4 (top)
Library of Congress, 12, 16; Manuscript Division/William Gobitas Papers, 23
National Archives and Records Administration (NARA), 13
North Wind Picture Archives, 7 (bottom)
"The Railroad Cut", Image courtesy of Gallon Historical Art, Gettysburg, PA, www.gallon.com, 10 (bottom)
Shutterstock/bluliq, 11 (top); disphotos, 10 (flag), 19 (flag); Dwight Smith, 6 (top)

Note: Essential content terms are **bold** and are defined at the bottom of the page where they first appear.

Table of Contents

CHAPTER 1

The Pledge of Allegiance
MAKING A PROMISE

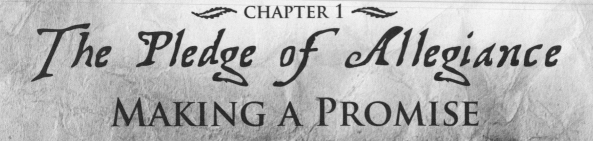

The **Pledge** of **Allegiance** is only 31 words long. You can probably say the pledge in less than 15 seconds. But next time, slow down. What are you really saying?

allegiance — loyalty

pledge — a promise

I pledge allegiance to my Flag and to the Republic for which it stands — One Nation indivisible — with liberty and justice for all

The pledge is a promise to respect your flag and your country. The members of the U.S. Congress make this promise each day before their meetings. Many state and local government leaders say the pledge too.

For more than 115 years, children have started the school day by saying the pledge. Most still do.

the original pledge as printed in 1892

SALUTE TO THE FLAG, by the Pupils.

At a signal from the Principal the pupils, in ordered ranks, hands to the side, face the Flag. Another signal is given; every pupil gives the Flag the military salute—right hand lifted, palm downward, to a line with the forehead and close to it. Standing thus, all repeat together, slowly : "I pledge allegiance to my Flag and the Republic for which it stands : one Nation indivisible, with Liberty and Justice for all." At the words, "to my Flag," the right hand is extended gracefully, palm upward, towards the Flag, and remains in this gesture till the end of the affirmation; whereupon all hands immediately drop to the side. Then, still standing, as the instruments strike a chord, all will sing AMERICA—"My Country, 'tis of Thee."

You might say it every day. But what does the Pledge of Allegiance really mean? Turn the page to find out.

CHAPTER 2

The Pledge of Allegiance
WHAT IT MEANS

The Pledge of Allegiance

I pledge allegiance to the flag of the
United States of America,

I pledge allegiance to my Flag and to the

Republic for which it stands — One Nation

indivisible — with liberty and justice for all

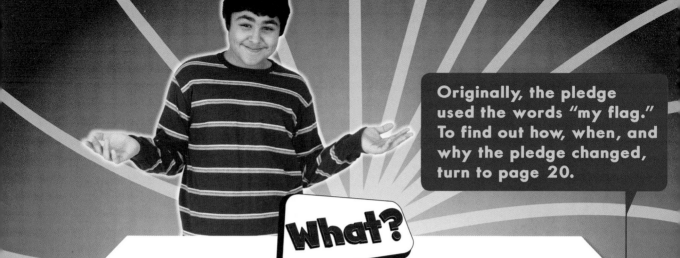

Originally, the pledge used the words "my flag." To find out how, when, and why the pledge changed, turn to page 20.

What?

I promise to be loyal to the **U.S. flag**.

Stars and Stripes

The U.S. flag hasn't always looked like it does now. At first, both a star and a stripe were added for each new state. But by 1818, there were 20 states. The flag was getting crowded. Congress decided the U.S. flag would have just 13 stripes to stand for the 13 original colonies. They also decided that the flag would have 20 stars, one for every

1794 flag with 15 stars and stripes

state. Each time a territory became a state, a new star was added. Today, there are 50 stars on the U.S. flag.

and to the **Republic** for which it stands,

U.S. Congress opens each new session by saying the pledge.

republic — a country in which the people elect their government leaders

The flag stands for the **United States of America**.

I also promise to be loyal to my country.

The United States is a republic. As an American, you have the right to elect your government's leaders.

Americans vote for their leaders in elections.

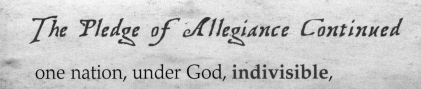

The Pledge of Allegiance Continued

one nation, under God, **indivisible**,

The Civil War tested the strength of the nation.

indivisible — not able to be divided

The United States has many states. But your promise of loyalty is to the entire country. You consider yourself an American first and a resident of your state second.

What?

The United States is a **strong country** that cannot be **divided**. We believe **God** watches over our nation.

The Civil War (1861–1865) tore families, friends, and the country apart. More than 620,000 Americans died of injuries or illnesses caused by the Civil War. But in the end, the United States came back together as a single nation.

This idea was added to the pledge in 1954. Find out why on page 21.

The Salute

Until 1924, people saluted the flag in a variety of ways. Most Americans saluted the flag with their right hands. At the words "my flag," they lifted their arms, palms up, toward the flag. The 1924 National Flag Conference suggested a change. Instead of saluting, people placed their hands over their hearts for the first part of the pledge. They still raised their hands at the word "flag." In 1942, Congress decided that people should keep their hands over their hearts throughout the pledge.

justice — fairness

liberty — freedom

In the United States, citizens have rights and **freedoms** guaranteed by the government. We have the right to be **treated fairly**. These freedoms belong to all Americans.

According to the Declaration of Independence, freedom is a basic right of all people.

The Declaration of Independence says that all men are created equal. Today, we would say "people" instead of "men."

IN CONGRESS. JULY 4, 1776.

The unanimous Declaration of the thirteen united States of America.

13

CHAPTER 3

The Pledge of Allegiance

THE STORY BEHIND THE PLEDGE

THE YOUTH'S COMPANION

Copyright, 1892, by

Vol. 65. No. 36.

BOSTON, THURSDAY

For the Companion.

THE LONE MOUNTAIN ROUTE.

There wasn't always a Pledge of Allegiance. The flag pledge first appeared in 1892 in a popular children's magazine called *Youth's Companion*. Each week, the magazine arrived in more than 450,000 mailboxes across the country. Its 12 pages were filled with news and stories for children.

Readers could earn prizes, called **premiums**, for selling the magazine to others. Premiums included toys, dolls, or writing paper.

pledge allegiance to my Flag and to the Republic for which it stands — One Nation indivisible — with liberty and justice for all

premium — prize

14

Free Flags

In 1888, *Youth's Companion* offered flags as premiums. At the time, few schools flew the United States flag. Flags were too expensive. Premiums were one way to earn flags. In 1891, *Youth's Companion* began offering flag certificates. Children sold the certificates for 10 cents each. After selling 100 certificates, they earned enough money to buy a flag for their school.

other premiums offered by *Youth's Companion*

Celebrating Columbus

James Upham ran *Youth's Companion*'s premium department. He thought children should learn to be good citizens. Upham decided to plan a celebration using the flags. The 400th anniversary of Christopher Columbus' arrival in America was coming up. Why not celebrate that?

Christopher Columbus landed in the West Indies on October 12, 1492.

James Upham

Youth's Companion asked children to hold a flag ceremony to honor Columbus. For the ceremony, children should fly the flag over their schools. Upham also thought children should say a flag pledge. He tried to write one, but he struggled. He gave the job to Francis Bellamy, who also worked in the premium department. Bellamy finished the pledge in about two hours. The pledge was printed in the September 8, 1892, copy of Youth's Companion.

Francis Bellamy

On October 21, 1892, schools around the country held Columbus Day celebrations. Newspapers reported thousands of flag ceremonies. The exact number is unknown, but as many as 12 million children said the flag pledge that day.

Pledge Laws

Upham and Bellamy thought the flag ceremony would be a one-time event. Others wanted schools to continue holding flag ceremonies. In 1898, New York passed a law requiring schools to display flags. The law also encouraged people to say the flag pledge. Other states passed flag laws in the early 1900s.

In 1919, the state of Washington required residents to hold weekly flag ceremonies. Washington's law also required students to say the flag pledge. A principal or teacher could be fired for failing to include the pledge. By 1935, about 10 states required students to salute the flag or say the pledge.

Today, most states require schools to begin the day with the Pledge of Allegiance. But students can choose whether they want to say the pledge or not.

Why Did the Pledge Change?

In the early 1900s, thousands of new immigrants came to the United States. Many of these people did not speak English. Their customs were different from those of most Americans. Americans expected the public schools to teach immigrant children what it means to be a U.S. citizen. A flag and the pledge were useful tools to teach good citizenship.

On June 14, 1923, representatives from the army, navy, and other groups held a National Flag Conference in Washington, D.C. The representatives discussed the flag pledge. Many people worried that the words "my flag" might remind new immigrants of their old countries. They voted to add the words "of the United States" to the pledge. The next year, the conference voted to add "of America" to make the message even clearer.

The flag pledge wasn't official until 1942. That year, Congress added it to the U.S. Flag Code. In 1945, the flag pledge became officially known as the Pledge of Allegiance.

During the 1950s, people in the United States worried about the spread of communism. Many communist governments restrict people's freedom to worship God. In 1954, the words "under God" were added to the pledge. These words reminded Americans that the United States was different from communist countries.

Protesting the Pledge

From the beginning, some Americans didn't like saying the flag pledge. However, few people complained until states required students to say the pledge. In 1911, the first protest came from a 14-year-old British girl living in New Jersey. She refused to say the pledge because her loyalty was to Great Britain. The next year a Canadian boy also protested.

The Gobitas family challenged the pledge laws on the basis of their religion.

During the 1920s and 1930s, more children refused to say the pledge. Sometimes, children were suspended from school or even taken away from their parents for refusing to say the pledge.

In the 1930s, the Gobitas family challenged the pledge. They argued that pledging to the flag was a form of worship. Worshiping the flag was against their religion. In 1940, the Supreme Court ruled that schools could require students to say the pledge.

But in 1943, the Supreme Court reversed that decision. The court said that each American is free to decide whether or not to say the pledge. Schools could no longer force students to say the pledge.

Minersville, Pa.
Nov. 5, 1935

Our School Directors
Dear Sirs
I do not salute the flag be
cause I have promised to do
the will of God. That means
that I must not worship anything
out of harmony with God's law.
In the twentieth chapter of
Exodus it is stated, "Thou shalt
not make unto thee any graven
image nor bow down to them nor
serve them for I the Lord thy God
am a jealous God visiting the in-
iquity of the fathers upon the children

Billy Gobitas wrote this letter to his school's director.

The Pledge Today

Recently, a California father went to court to have the words "under God" removed from the Pledge of Allegiance. He did not want his daughter to hear the pledge, even if she didn't have to say it. At first, the Court of Appeals agreed. But the Supreme Court later overturned that ruling. In 2002, Congress passed a law approving the current wording of the Pledge of Allegiance. The law says that the words "under God" belong in the pledge.

For many citizens, saying the pledge is a way to show they love their country. Most schools begin the day with the Pledge of Allegiance. Anyone who does not want to join in may sit quietly until the pledge is finished. One of the strengths of the United States is the freedom it gives its citizens to disagree. When you respect that freedom, you respect your country.

The pledge is different today than it was in 1892. But you may still recite the pledge's 31 words in school, during meetings, and at special ceremonies. Even though the pledge is short, its words are full of meaning.

Time Line

Youth's Companion begins a program to place a flag in every schoolhouse.

Schoolchildren say the Pledge of Allegiance during the first Columbus Day celebration.

1888

October 21, 1892

September 8, 1892

August 1892

1923

Francis Bellamy writes the Pledge of Allegiance.

The National Flag Conference changes "my Flag" to "the Flag of the United States."

Youth's Companion publishes the Pledge of Allegiance.

The National Flag Conference adds "of America" to the pledge.

Congress adds the words "under God" to the pledge.

1924

1954

1943

1942

2002

Congress officially recognizes the Pledge of Allegiance.

Congress passes a bill approving the current wording of the Pledge of Allegiance, in particular the words "under God."

The Supreme Court rules that students cannot be forced to recite the pledge.

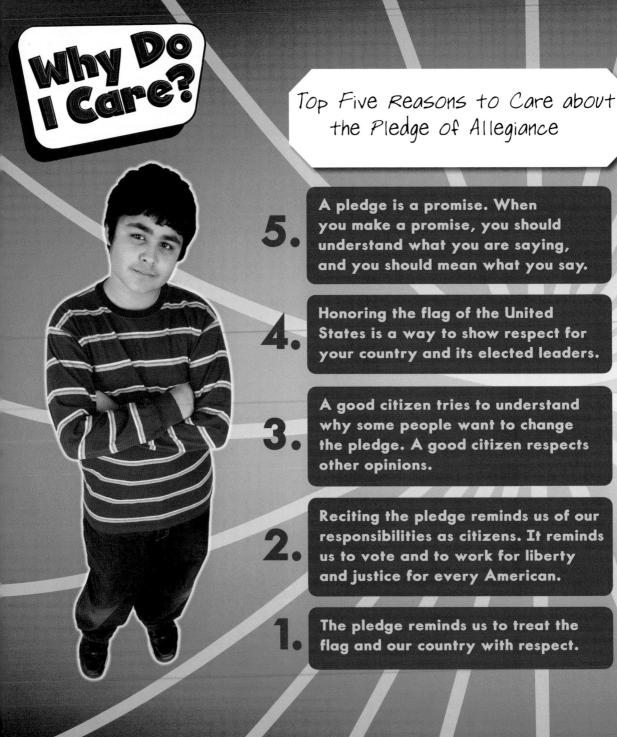

Why Do I Care?

Top Five Reasons to Care about the Pledge of Allegiance

5. A pledge is a promise. When you make a promise, you should understand what you are saying, and you should mean what you say.

4. Honoring the flag of the United States is a way to show respect for your country and its elected leaders.

3. A good citizen tries to understand why some people want to change the pledge. A good citizen respects other opinions.

2. Reciting the pledge reminds us of our responsibilities as citizens. It reminds us to vote and to work for liberty and justice for every American.

1. The pledge reminds us to treat the flag and our country with respect.

allegiance — Is an allegiance a group of superheroes? No, allegiance means you have loyalty and respect for something, like the flag or the country.

indivisible — Put away your calculators. This isn't a math problem. When something is indivisible, it can't be split up or broken into pieces.

justice — Have you ever heard of the Justice League? In the pledge, justice means fairness, especially when it comes to the law.

liberty — Simply put, liberty means freedom. In the United States, you have many rights and freedoms under the law.

pledge — We're not talking about the cleaning product. A pledge is an oath or promise.

Glossary

allegiance (uh-LEE-junss) — loyalty and obedience owed to one's country or government

communism (KOM-yuh-niz-uhm) — a way of organizing a country so that all the land, houses, factories, and other property belong to the government or community, and the profits are shared by all

immigrant (IM-uh-gruhnt) — someone who comes from one country to live permanently in another country

indivisible (in-duh-VIS-uh-buhl) — not able to be divided

justice (JUHSS-tiss) — fair behavior or treatment

liberty (LIB-ur-tee) — freedom

pledge (PLEJ) — a promise or agreement that must be kept; to pledge means to make a sincere promise.

premium (PREE-mee-uhm) — a prize or reward for doing something such as selling magazines

republic (ri-PUHB-lik) — a country that has a form of government in which people elect representatives to manage the government

Sites

FactHound offers a safe, fun way to find Internet sites related to this book. All of the sites on FactHound have been researched by our staff.

Here's how:

1. Visit *www.facthound.com*

2. Choose your grade level.

3. Type in this book ID **1429619317** for age-appropriate sites. You may also browse subjects by clicking on letters, or by clicking on pictures and words.

4. Click on the **Fetch It** button.

FactHound will fetch the best sites for you!

Read More

Fata, Heather. *The Pledge of Allegiance.* A Primary Source Library of American Citizenship. New York: Rosen Central Primary Source, 2004.

Pearl, Norman. *The Pledge of Allegiance.* American Symbols. Minneapolis: Picture Window Books, 2007.

Silate, Jennifer. *The American Flag.* Primary Sources of American Symbols. New York: PowerKids Press, 2006.

Tourville, Amanda Doering. *The Pledge of Allegiance.* Edina, Minn.: Magic Wagon, 2008.

Index